The Gutenberg Bible

*A sixteenth-century idea of
Gutenberg's appearance (A. Thevet,
Pourtraits et vies, 1584)*

The Gutenberg Bible

Martin Davies

Pomegranate Artbooks • San Francisco

in association with

THE BRITISH LIBRARY

sentenciaꝝ grauitate referte ! ut utꝝ utri
laude ꝓferat·iudicare sit difficile·Prętereo
quæ de galliæ hyspaniæꝗ prestantia soluta
oratione scripsisti·Nō eni est huius tēporis,de
tuis studiis,ꝓsertim ad te scribere·De studi/
oꝝ humanitatis restitutōe loquor· Quibus
(quātū ipse coniectura capio)magnū lumē no
uoꝝ librarioꝝ genus attulit·quos nōa me/
moria(sicut qdam equus troianus)quoquo/
uerso effudit germania·Ferūt eni illic,haut
procul a ciuitate Maguncia, Ioannē quendā
fuisse,cui cognomē bonemōtano.q ꝓmus oīm
impressoriā arte excogitauerit·q̄ nō calamo

(ut prisci qdem illi)neꝗ penna(ut nos fin
gimus)sed æreis lris libri fingunt·& qdem
expedite,polite,& pulchre·Dignus sane hic
uir fuit!q̄ omēs musæ,omēs artes,oīsꝗ eoꝝ
linguæ,q libris delectant! diuinis laudibꝰ
ornent· eoꝗ magis dis,deabusꝗ anteponāt!
quo ꝓpius ac ꝓsentius lris ipsis,ac studiosis
homībus,suffragiū tulit· Si qdem deificant
liber & alma ceres·ille qꝓpe dona lici inue
nit, poculaꝗ inuētis acheloia miscuit uuis.
hæc chaoniam pingui glandem mutauit ari/
sta·Atꝗ(ut poeta utamur altero)prima ce/

THE GUTENBERG BIBLE is the first Western printed book of any length and one of the few old books known by name to the general public, rivalled in this regard only by the first Folio of Shakespeare. Yet the inventor of printing, Johann Gutenberg, has left not one identifiable word of his own in print or handwriting, except for a document issued in pursuance of a debt years before he took up printing. None of the few books which scholarship has assigned to his press carries his name. His career is almost entirely a matter for conjecture, with only one or two fixed points to anchor speculation: the undisputed facts concerning him could be easily set down on a single sheet of paper. The documents which explicitly mention Gutenberg are either the outcome of court cases brought against him, partial in themselves and difficult to interpret, or the banal records of his involvement in everyday legal or financial transactions. None gives any insight into his character or motivation. Of the nearly thirty documents that survive in originals or copies from his lifetime, only two make any mention of printing. It is possible to read quite detailed accounts of his movements and activities, even of his outlook on life, which have no foundation in any testimony that has reached us. Many theories can be poured into the huge gaps in the evidence, and few can be refuted with absolute confidence. A

I
The first printed notice naming Gutenberg ('Ioannes nemontanus') the inventor of printing: Gasparino Barzizza, rthographia, Paris 1471

thoroughgoing scepticism in the face of these gaps is the healthiest attitude. About Gutenberg we know in truth very little more than when his name was first mentioned in print, in a book of 1471 from the first printers of France (Fig. 1):

There was near Mainz a certain Johann surnamed Gutenberg, who was the very first man to devise the art of printing by which books were not written, as they used to be, with a reed nor with a pen as we do now, but by metal characters, and that with speed, elegance and beauty.

More solid but hardly easier to interpret is the evidence of the great work with which his name is forever connected: the book of almost 1,300 large-format pages now called the Gutenberg Bible, known to a previous age from one of its owners as the Mazarine Bible and to bibliographers as the 42-line Bible. This is universally agreed to have been printed by him in the German city of Mainz in the middle of the fifteenth century. Printing from blocks and from movable type was known in the Far East long before Gutenberg but for a variety of reasons, social and political rather than technological, the invention never had the profound impact it was to have in Germany and the rest of Europe. The Gutenberg Bible is the harbinger and exemplar of the half millennium from which we are only now emerging, an age dominated by the radical consequences of printing from movable metal types.

The Bible is, besides, the central text of the religion of the West, the book of books, the source of faith and its palpable expression. In its earliest printing it is also, in the opinion of many critics, one of the most beautiful books ever produced.

'Golden Mainz', *Aurea Moguntia*, on the confluence of the Main and the Rhine not far from Frankfurt, was one of the most important cities of the Holy Roman Empire (Fig. 2). It was a free imperial city, for a long time effectively under the governance of its archbishop, who was by tradition the first elector of the emperor and chancellor of the empire. His court was staffed by high officials who came to form a patrician class in the city. A thriving industrial life led in Mainz, as in other medieval cities, to the organization of craftsmens' guilds, for the cloth trades, for example, or the working of gold. In Gutenberg's time these guilds often found themselves in opposition to the patricians in the struggle for local political control and commercial advantage. As far as can be determined, Gutenberg's own background was on three sides patrician, but his maternal grandfather on the fourth had been a shopkeeper and guild-member.

Gutenberg thus started life, in Mainz towards the end of the fourteenth century, with a complicated and conflicting inheritance. Like other Mainz patricians, his father took his surname from the family house in the city, the Hof zum

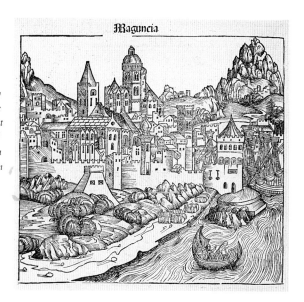

2
Mainz in a contemporary woodcut. The view is in fact a generalized depiction of a medieval town on a river (Nuremberg Chronicle, 1493)

Gutenberg. His full name appears in documents as Friele Gensfleisch zur Laden zum Gutenberg, and his eldest son was also called Friele. Our Gutenberg (see Frontispiece), often referred to by local or diminutive forms of Johann such as Hans, Henne or Henchin, was the youngest child, having besides his brother Friele an elder sister, named Else after her mother. Calculations from the lives of the two elder children enable the date of birth of Johann Gensfleisch zum Gutenberg —

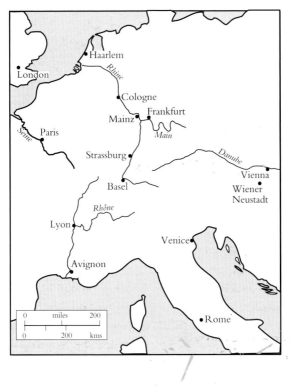

3
Mainz at the centre of fifteenth-century Europe

John Gooseflesh of the Good Mountain — to be roughly fixed in the period 1394-99.

Nothing is known of Gutenberg's schooling or whether

he received any form of higher education. He may well have attended a local school, possibly at the monastic foundation of St Victor in Mainz, where at the end of his life he was a member of a lay brotherhood. He would have acquired the rudiments of Latin through an abbreviated version of the ancient Roman grammar known as Donatus. This had been the staple diet of schoolchildren throughout the Middle Ages and was to become by far the most frequently printed book in the fifteenth century. To judge from the surviving fragments, there is a good chance that Donatus was actually the first text ever printed, as Gutenberg experimented with the new technique in preparation for the Bible.

All that lay in the future, at the beginning of the 1450s. The first records of the historical Gutenberg date from the late 1420s and early 1430s. He is twice mentioned in connection with the transfer of annuities, a form of investment income backed by the city treasury on which many Mainz patricians depended. The second of these documents, dated January 1430, suggests that Gutenberg was no longer resident in Mainz, and the new constitution of the city drawn up later that year to reconcile a group of exiled patricians with the city council of guildsmen specially names him as one of the exiles who were now to be allowed to return. Gutenberg must have been among the patricians expelled in 1428 when the guilds

succeeded in ousting them from their civic privileges.

It is doubtful that he returned in 1430, for there is no trace of him in Mainz for another nineteen years. Instead he next appears a hundred miles to the south, up the valley of the Rhine at the great imperial city of Strassburg, at that time a wholly German settlement. He emerges there in March 1434 in full vigour, pursuing a claim for an unpaid annuity against the city of Mainz, for which he had apparently had the Mainz city clerk imprisoned. It is in the nature of the sort of documents that survive to offer a dark picture of Gutenberg's financial dealings, but he does in truth seem to have had lifelong troubles in this department. We might also draw from this particular document conclusions about Gutenberg's pugnacity and tenaciousness of purpose. Those certainly are the qualities in evidence in the most important of the Strassburg records, the Dritzehn lawsuit.

The original record of the suit is lost. It has been partly preserved in later copies of several different entries in Strassburg registers which are now destroyed. Most of the extant portion relates the evidence of witnesses for and against Gutenberg, though on both sides the reports are incomplete. The legal judgment which concluded the case was issued at the end of 1439 as the result of a rather complicated set of circumstances. In essence we find Gutenberg in dispute with

the brothers of a man whom he had taken into two successive partnerships. The first partnership was to teach their brother, Andreas Dritzehn, the art of polishing gemstones. Some time later, perhaps three or four years later, Gutenberg and Andreas Dritzehn joined with two other inhabitants of Strassburg to work on 'an art to be used on the occasion of the pilgrimage to Aachen'. This, it appears, was an enterprise to make small hand-mirrors. Pilgrims would use the mirrors to catch the image and hence the power of relics displayed periodically at the great shrine of Aachen, or Aix-la-Chapelle, the old imperial capital of Charlemagne. Unfortunately, the partners had misjudged the year in which the pilgrimage was due to take place, which was not 1439 but 1440.

At this juncture the associates turned to Gutenberg and asked him to instruct them in any further arts that he might have 'discovered or otherwise knew'. On this basis a further agreement for a five-year partnership was drawn up; but very soon, at Christmas 1438, Andreas Dritzehn died, in great distress of mind and with his affairs in considerable confusion. His two brothers now required Gutenberg to admit them to the partnership in his place. Since Andreas had not paid his full share at the time of his death, however, and since the original agreement had a clause which specifically provided that the tools and products were to remain in the partnership

in the event of the death of any of the partners, Gutenberg repeatedly refused either to admit them or to refund them more than a small proportion of Andreas's investment. And the court backed him up.

The court reports are fragmentary and obscure, but a number of details in the testimony of the opposing sides have aroused much interest and speculation. Andreas Dritzehn had evidently put a great deal of money into some technical process from which a good profit could be foreseen but which—in an age before patents and copyright—it was desired to keep secret. The terms include *formen*, forms, later signifying letters or types, *pressen*, a press, and certain 'pieces' (*stücke*) which apparently fitted together to make some implement central to the process and which Gutenberg wanted to have dismantled when Andreas was on his deathbed. One witness even mentions that he had received 100 guilders as early as 1436 for work that 'concerned only *trucken*'. This word means 'to impress' and in the modern period 'to print'.

Scholars have naturally taken these tantalizing indications as pointing to experimentation with the printing of books. It is difficult to resist this view, but there are in fact grave, if not conclusive, objections. All of the terms used in the evidence could have been applied to (say) a new process for mass-producing frames for the pilgrim mirrors, contem-

porary examples of which survive today. Gutenberg's five-year partnership continued, so far as we know, with the remaining Strassburg partners, yet the results were not sufficiently promising to induce any of the partners to seek to renew it. Above all, despite intensive searching for the earliest evidence of printing, nothing has survived that can be plausibly associated even with the 1440s, let alone the 1430s. We do have a sequence of very early fragments which can be taken back no further than the first years of the 1450s: what, then, was going on in 1436? The sequence can be coherently ordered by the progressive refinement of the printing types and presswork, and this typographical development accords with the chronological framework suggested by the one document certainly concerned with Gutenberg's activities at the printing press, another court record drawn up at the end of 1455. If looked at without the prejudice inevitably brought by hindsight, the Strassburg documents by no means impose the conclusion that Gutenberg was engaged there in typographic printing. And if he was, the experiment failed, we must suppose for want of funds, and all material trace of it has been lost.

Gutenberg crops up occasionally in the Strassburg tax registers until early 1444, variously associated with the city aristocracy and with the goldsmith's guild there, though as a

non-citizen he could be a full member of neither. He was in the unusual position of carrying on the handiwork of an artisan with the status of a patrician. Only one other detail is known of his stay in Strassburg, in the summary of a lawsuit in which he was sued for breach of promise of marriage. The original record, like so many others connected with Gutenberg, has disappeared; but the lady involved, the wonderfully named Ennelin zu der Yserin Thüre — Little Anne of the Iron Doors — was to all appearances unsuccessful. As far as we know Gutenberg remained unmarried all his days. From 12 March 1444 until he is found once again at Mainz in October 1448, his activities are a complete blank. Various fact-finding missions have been dreamed up to fill the gap, to Haarlem in Holland or to Avignon in the south of France, both sites of experiments with printing according to later report.

Once Gutenberg was back in Mainz, however, we can reconstruct the course of his affairs with greater assurance. This is very largely thanks to the single vellum sheet in the University Library of Göttingen which is known as the Helmasperger Instrument. In 1455 the notary Dr Ulrich Helmasperger supplied this summary of the proceedings against Gutenberg to the person who had brought the suit against him, Johann Fust, citizen and lawyer of Mainz. The

Instrument is formally the record (in difficult German dialect) of an oath taken by Fust on 6 November 1455. The tale it tells is clear enough in its general outlines, though very different interpretations have been placed on it.

The story begins with Gutenberg's return to Mainz, which we learn about from a contract signed by a relative of his on 17 October 1448. The document guaranteed that Johann would repay the interest and principal of a loan of 150 Rhenish guilders. This was a relatively modest figure in relation to his real needs in setting up what must by this time have been a printing office. He soon found in the rich lawyer Fust a steadier backer, though as it turned out one with neither a bottomless pocket nor endless patience. The Helmasperger Instrument records the very substantial sums that passed from Fust to Gutenberg and the corresponding deterioration in their relations.

About 1450 Gutenberg received from Fust a loan of 800 guilders to provide equipment, no doubt for his printing office. The equipment itself was to serve as security for the loan, which carried interest at six per cent. Later a second sum of 800 guilders was advanced by Fust on condition that he was taken on as a partner in 'the work of the books', the investment to be used 'for the profit of both'. This second 800 guilders either incorporated or superseded an arrangement

whereby Fust was to pay the running costs — food, wages, rent — for the common enterprise at the rate of 300 guilders per annum. On this understanding the work, not here more precisely specified, continued until 1455, when Fust launched these proceedings for the recovery both of the principal of 1600 guilders and of a total of 426 guilders in interest. As a result of Gutenberg's failure to adhere to the agreement, Fust claimed, he had had to make the interest payments on the second 800 guilders, which he himself had been obliged to borrow. The oath that Fust had to swear, which provides the reason for the document we have, was to confirm that he had in fact borrowed this money. A great deal of money was involved: a master craftsman might earn 20 or 30 guilders a year, a German town-house built in stone would cost perhaps 80 or 100 guilders.

It seems that the court ordered Gutenberg to reimburse Fust for the original loan of 800 guilders and as much of the second 800 guilders as had not been spent on their common work, plus the 426 guilders interest. It is unknown what steps Gutenberg took to meet this judgement, but it is fairly clear that he was not in a position to pay such large sums. It is accordingly assumed, no doubt correctly, that the printing equipment—purchased with the same loan for which it stood as security—was seized by Fust in settlement of the original

loan of five years earlier.

It has long been seen that the Latin Bible now associated with his name is the chief work for which Gutenberg was seeking these considerable sums — printing has always required large capital investment before sales can bring a return. A copy in the Bibliothèque Nationale in Paris was finished by hand in August 1456 (Fig. 4), and there is no book other than the Bible which will answer the requirements of the Helmasperger Instrument in terms of scale or chronology. The Instrument was always likely to remain an isolated witness to the circumstances of the Bible's production, but recently attention has been drawn to an astonishingly precise notice of the Bible in the making, and that from a wholly unexpected quarter.

Aeneas Sylvius Piccolomini, offspring of a noble family of Siena in Tuscany, was a humanist in the Renaissance sense — a literary man, schooled in the classics. After many twists and turns he became Pope Pius II in 1458. Before that he had led an exciting, at times rather irregular life as a diplomat and courtier of kings and popes. He had spent much time north of the Alps, acting successively in the interests of the Council of Basel (an anti-papal meeting of clerics), of Emperor Frederick III of Germany, and following reconciliation with the Church of Rome, of Pope Nicholas V. A meeting of German princes and prelates to address the urgent threat posed

4
The rubricator's notice in the Paris Bibliothèque Nationale paper copy, stating that the rubrication was finished on 24 August 1456 (St Bartholomew's Day)

...n tymbalis benesonantibus. lauda
re cui ctalis iubilationis: ois spirit[us]
laudet dum. Alla. Alleluia

Et sic est finis prime partis biblie
scz veteris testamenti Illuminata
seu rubricata et ligata p henricum
Albch alias cremer Anno dm ...
lvi festo Bartholomei apli

Deo gracias . Alleluia

by the Turkish advance into Europe was held at Frankfurt, some forty miles from Mainz, on 15-28 October 1454. The proceedings were opened by an address from Aeneas Sylvius. A few months later, in March 1455, he sent a long Latin letter from Wiener Neustadt (the Emperor's capital near Vienna) relating the political situation to a friend and fellow prelate, the Spanish Cardinal Juan de Carvajal. The short passage on the Bible, casually inserted amid the political news, reads in translation as follows:

All that has been written to me about that marvellous man seen at Frankfurt is true. I have not seen complete Bibles but only a number of quires of various books of the Bible. The script was very neat and legible, not at all difficult to follow — your grace would be able to read it without effort, and indeed without glasses. Several people told me that 158 copies have been finished, though others say there are 180. I'm not certain of the exact number but I'm in no doubt that the volumes *are* finished, if my informants are to be trusted.

If I had known your wishes I should certainly have bought you a copy — some quires have even been brought here to the Emperor. I shall try and see if I can have a copy for sale brought here which I can purchase on your behalf. But I fear that won't be possible, both because of the length of the journey and because buyers were said to be lined up even before the books were finished. I can deduce your grace's great desire to know how matters stand from the fact that the messenger you sent was quicker than Pegasus! But that's enough joking.

This letter, which evidently follows up previous correspondence now lost to us, was brought to students' attention from manuscripts as recently as 1982, but it has in fact been in print, in a rare edition of Pius II's letters, for more than 500 years (Fig. 5). The entirely offhand information it gives — Aeneas Sylvius has much more important things on his mind — accords remarkably well with some conclusions derived from previous study of the Bible, at the same time excluding others. It also shifts the focus from the inventor — if we take 'that marvellous man' to be Gutenberg — to the invention. And to the invention of printing itself we now turn before attempting to match the evidence of the documents to that of the book as we have it.

We shall probably never know the motives or inspiration that turned Gutenberg to 'the art of multiplying books', to use one of the early terms for printing. Behind the whole process lay large social and technical developments, notably a great growth of literacy and education; a corresponding wide spread of institutions and people possessed of the means to afford, and the time to devote to, reading matter on a large scale; a growth in standardization of texts and hence the need to multiply them in identical copies (Aeneas Sylvius's friend, the German Cardinal Nicholas of Cusa, had ordered the writing

et si morem suū tenuit seraginta tamē dieb9 ante fes
tū purificationis aut saltē quiquaginta Roman petijt
itaqz nō deerat tempus designādi legati etiaz cardina
lis ꞇ maxime cū se tam voluntariū morosieñ offerret
ego illius promptidinē laudo q̃ p̃ fide catholica tanto
labori p̃sonā suā nō denegat neqz ordinis vestru ferre
sardñā si iubeatur recusat q̃uis multi morosieñ inue
niri possent nisi rutem Vox illa impedimento essz que
vulgo fertur pater sancte non plura cardinalia de vi
ro illo mirabili apud frācfordiam viso · nihil falsi ad
me scriptuz est non vidi Biblias integras sed quiter
niones aliquot diuersorum librorum mundissime ac
correctissime littere nulla i p̃te mendaces q̃s tua dig
natio sine labore ꞇ absqz berillo legeret Volumina vē
tū ꞇ quiq̃gintaocto absoluta esse ex pluribus testib9 di
dici q̃uis aliq̃ ꞇētū ꞇ octogita eē confirmauerit de nūo
mihi nō plane ꞇstat de p̃scd voluminū si fides hñda ē
hoib9 nō sū dubi9 si sciuissez desiderii tuū · emisse ē vnū p̃
aul dubio volumē · q̃terniones eē aliq̃t t ad cesatē de
lati s̄t conabor si poterit fieri aliq̃ huc bibliā venalem
afferri eamqz tui cū cōparo qd timeo ne fieri possit · et
p̃pter distātiā itineris · et q̃ añq̃ p̃sicerent volumia
p̃ratos emptores fuisse tradunt q̃ autē tua dignatio
magnope desiderauerit · huj9 ꞇi ꞇctitudiez hr̄o inde conijcio

out of thousands of identical indulgences in aid of the crusade in the early 1450s); finally, a high degree of skill in metal-working and an entrepreneurial atmosphere where substantial capital sums might be placed at risk without prospect of a quick return.

The more immediate sources of inspiration are equally elusive. Forms of reproducing determinate shapes by impression, such as lettering on leather bindings or woodcut designs inked and transferred by rubbing on to paper, were everywhere to be seen but could hardly suggest the solution to the problem of mechanical reproduction of script. And even supposing Gutenberg saw a sample of Eastern printing, for which there is no evidence, he could never have deduced his method from the bulky ideograms, each recurring only occasionally, there set down on paper. With the Roman alphabet the problem is different: how to manipulate economically and with exact alignment very large quantities of a limited number of very small signs — as small as marks of punctuation — constantly repeated in changing combinations.

The solution Gutenberg found did not alter in its essentials for nearly four hundred years, until the age of the machine press. At the heart of the invention was the type-casting instrument. The first stage was to engrave the letter forms onto iron punches which were hammered into slips of

5
The first mention of the Bible, in a letter of Pius II dated 12 March 1455 (Epistolae, Cologne, about 1480)

softer metal called matrices: these then showed the sunken impression of the letter. The type-casting instrument was a hinged mould which could be adjusted to the exact size of the letter required — wider for an m, narrower for an i, for example. Molten typemetal was poured into the mould in which sat the matrix bearing the punched impression of the letter. A quick shake filled the internal channels and the typemetal — mostly lead, with tin and antimony added for fluidity and hardness — would then set solid almost at once. The mould was opened and out dropped a stalk of metal bearing at the end the reversed image in relief of the character. With care and a minimum of skill thousands of identical types could thus be produced, all carefully dressed to produce an even height when locked in a frame, or 'forme' (Fig. 6).

6

The type used in the Bible: a modern reconstruction in the Gutenberg Museum, Mainz

After this breakthrough the mechanics of setting the inked frame of type to paper with the aid of a press were relatively simple. We do not have examples of printing presses from Gutenberg's time but some from the second half of the next century do survive in Antwerp. They conform to the pattern seen in the single known illustration of a fifteenth-century press, a Lyonnese *Danse macabre*, or Dance of Death, the only copy of which is in the British Library (Fig. 7). The reconstruction of a press of the time in the Gutenberg-Museum at Mainz shows the folding frame on a carriage (Fig. 8).

Mors resecat/mors omne necat quod carne creatur / Magnificos premit:z modicos/cunctis dominatur.

Nobilium tenet imperium nulli reueretur: / Tam ducibus qz principibz commune habetur.

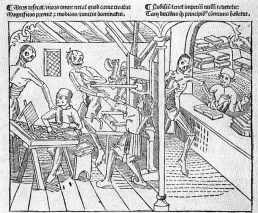

7

The only known picture of a fifteenth-century printing press: a woodcut in the Danse Macabre, *Lyon, 1500 (BL IB.41735)*

8

A reconstruct[ion] of Gutenbe[rg's] workshop (Gutenbe[rg] Museum, Mainz)

Nunc vbi ius/vbi leg/vbi voy/vbi flos inuenitur. hic nisi pus/nisi feis/nisi terre precio vilis.

Le mort

Venez danser vng tourdion
Imprimeurs sus legierement
Venez tost/pour conclusion
Mourir vous fault certainement
Faictes vng sault habillement
Presses/z caspes vous fault laisser
Reculer ny fault nullement
A sommage on congnoist loutier.

Les imprimeurs

Helas on aurons nous recours
Puis que la mort nous espie
Imprime auons tous les cours
De la saincte theologie
Loix/decret/z poeterie
Par nre art plusieurs sont grans clers
Reuelee en est clergie
Les vouloirs des gens sont diuers

Le mort

Sus auant vous tres apres
Maistre libraire marchez auant
Vous me regardez de bien pres
Laissez voz liures maintenant
Danser vous fault/a quel galant
Mettez icy voftre pensee
Comment vous reculez marchant
Comencement nest pas fusee

Le libraire

Me fault il maulgre moy danser
Je croy que ouy/mort me presse
Et me contraint de me auancer
Nesse pas dure destresse
Des liures il fault que ie laisse
Et ma boutique desormais
Dont ie pers toute lyesse
Tel est blece qui ney peult mais.

6

This took the paper to be printed over the locked-up forme of type and under the plate of the press, or platen. By a pull of the bar the platen would be made to descend firmly and evenly onto the paper and press it onto the inked type.

The engraving of the steel punches, along with the crucial invention of the type-casting equipment itself, is reckoned to be one of Gutenberg's own special contributions. The inked type impressions we see as print are certainly the result of long and patient development: they attempt with considerable success to render in rigid metal the organic forms of German handwriting of the time. The style of writing found in the 42-line Bible is called 'textura', a large gothic hand traditionally used for biblical, liturgical and school texts alike — the first printer at Cologne later said that Gutenberg started with 'Missal types' (full-size reproductions are seen in Figs 9-10, the passage of St Luke concerning the Annunciation and the opening of St John's Gospel). In the hands of a skilled scribe, such as Gutenberg's assistant Peter Schöffer, the letters varied subtly but systematically according to their position in the word or line. The object was to equalize the distance between the vertical strokes of the letters and thus to present the 'woven' appearance which gives the script its name *textura*. It is this variability of form which caused the earliest printers, who naturally aimed to offer the public books

Et ingressus ãgelus ad eã dixit. Aue
gratia plena:dñs tecũ:benedicta tu in
mulieribꝫ. Que tũ audisset·turbata est
in sermone eius : et cogitabat qualis
esset ista salutatio . Et ait angelus ei
Ne timeas maria: inuenisti etũ grati
am apud deũ. Ecce concipies in utero
et paries filiũ:ꝝ uocabis nomen eius
iħesum.Hic erit magnus:ꝝ fili⁹ altissi
mi uocabitur. Et dabit illi dñs de⁹ se
dem dauid patris eius : et regnabit ĩ
domo iacob in eternũ : et regni ei⁹ nõ
erit finis. Dixit aũt maria ad angelũ.
Quomõ fiet istud : quoniã uirũ non
cognosco? Et respõdens angelus di
xit ei . Spiritus sanctus superueniet in
te:ꝝ uirtus altissimi obumbrabit tibi.
Ideoꝗ et qõ nascet ex te sanctũ : uoca
bit fili⁹ dei. Et ecce elizabeth cognata tu
a:ꝝ ipa cõcepit filiũ ĩ senectute sua . Et
hic mẽsis est sext⁹ illi q̃ uocat sterilis?

N principio erat verbū : ⁊ verbū erat
apud deū : et de⁹ erat verbū. Hoc erat
in principio apud deū. Omnia p ipm
facta sunt: ⁊ sine ipo factum est nichil
Quod factū est in ipo vita erat:⁊ vita
erat lux hominū: et lux in tenebris lu
cet · ⁊ tenebre eā nō comphenderūt . Fu
it homo missus a deo: cui nomē erat io
hānes. Hic venit ī testimoniū ut testi
moniū phiberet de lumine : ut omnes
crederent p illū. Nō erat ille lux: sed ut
testimoniū phiberet de lumine . Erat
lux vera : que illuminat omnē homi
nem venientem in hūc mundū. In mū
do erat:⁊ mūdus p ipm factus est : et
mūdus eū non cognouit. In ppria ve
nit: ⁊ sui eū nō receperūt . Quotqt aūt
receperūt eū · dedit eis potestatem filios
dei fieri: hijs qui credūt in nomine ei⁹.
Qui nō ex sanguinibz neqz ex volun
tate carnis · neqz ex volūtate viri : sed
ex deo nati sunt . Et verbū caro factum
est lahitauit in nois . Et vidimus

which resembled as closely as possible contemporary manuscripts, to manufacture such a large set of characters — in the case of the Gutenberg Bible getting on for 300 separate letter forms (see the abbreviated conspectus in Fig. 11).

Fragments of more than twenty different editions of the schoolbook Donatus in this type, as well an indulgence partly printed with it in 1454, show what common sense in any case suggests, that the perfection of the Bible was won by long experiment and did not spring fully formed from the mind of the inventor. But there is a more extensive series of schoolbooks, another edition of the same indulgence, several calendars and other popular texts in the vernacular, and even another Bible, all printed in a quite different type, undoubtedly for the most part at Mainz in the 1450s. It is the existence of this variant textura type, known from its regular vehicles as the Donatus-Kalender or D-K type, that is the hardest problem of Gutenberg studies. There is a clear line of development in the D-K type, culminating in the production of a second Bible. This 36-line Bible, which was demonstrably set up from a copy of the 42-line Bible, was almost certainly printed at the end of the 1450s not at Mainz but at Bamberg in Bavaria, where we find the type in use by a printer named Albrecht Pfister in the early 1460s. Yet the Mainz versions of this type are in their earliest manifestations more

10
The opening of St John's Gospel: 'In the beginning was the word'
(BL C.9.d.4)

II

A specimen conspectus of the types used in the Gutenberg Bible

primitive than, and probably predate, the 42-line Bible type, which seems consciously designed as an improvement. Nothing in either series bears a date, though several pieces, including the two indulgences, are datable to 1454.

The alternatives are stark indeed. Either the D-K type

belongs to an unknown printer of whom history has nothing to say, or Gutenberg was the originator of both series of types. The second view is now gaining ground, if only for horror of a vacuum. The argument runs: who else could have made type in that primordial stage, apparently earlier even than any surviving witness of the 42-line Bible type? In that form the argument is not very compelling. It may be legitimately inferred from the Helmasperger Instrument, however, that Gutenberg was printing independently of his joint work with Fust. Biographers have combined this deduction with speculation that a Mainz printing house later (in 1481) in the hands of Peter Schöffer and in the 1450s owned by a distant relative of Gutenberg may have been the site of the printing establishment run by Gutenberg in partnership with Johann Fust. In that case the two houses, Schöffer's Hof zum Humbrecht and the Hof zum Gutenberg, could have been responsible for the production of the parallel series of Donatuses and indulgences, one as common work of the partnership and the other on Gutenberg's own account. The latter enterprise would then have been devoted to the manufacture of ephemera — indulgences and so on — and easily sold schooltexts in the D-K type. This type was perhaps at that stage found to be unsuitable for the big Bible which was the object of the partnership as being too greedy of expensive

paper and vellum — the fewer the lines of type that could be fitted on to the page, the larger the number of sheets needed to accommodate the text. It has to be stressed that this reconstruction is highly conjectural and that we have no definite evidence of the location of any press worked by Gutenberg.

What is undisputed is that the 'work of the books' was the joint enterprise of Fust and Gutenberg to make the 42-line Bible and that this is the very book that was seen at Frankfurt, perhaps at the congress of October 1454. At that stage it was still uncompleted — Aeneas Sylvius is explicit on the point — and consisted, as far as could be seen, of various quires (gatherings of five sheets, or ten leaves, or twenty pages) from different books of the Bible. By the time of his letter to Carvajal of 12 March 1455, Aeneas Sylvius has been informed on certain authority that the book was complete. In the meantime, it appears, loose quires had been brought to show to Emperor Frederick III. We may therefore place the completion of the Bible at the turn of 1454-55, in time for the news to reach Wiener Neustadt from Mainz, some 400 miles away, by early March. Aeneas Sylvius is also helpful — more helpful than he knew — on the exact number of copies printed.

It has long been clear from analysis of different copies of the Bible that the size of the edition was at a certain point

increased. Early printers never maintained large stocks of type: the custom was to have enough in the typesetter's case for setting up perhaps four or five pages. Once all the copies of a page had been printed off the type would be distributed back into the typecase. When, therefore, the decision was taken to increase the edition size — we can see now from Aeneas Sylvius's letter that this was probably in view of heavy advance demand — those quires which had been printed off would already have had their type distributed and freshly set-up sheets would need to be printed to bring those quires up to the number now required. That this happened at the end of the main print run allows us to see both the earliest and latest stages of the technique as it developed in the long period — perhaps as much as two years — that the Bible was at the press.

There are thus two 'editions' of certain quires, though the mixture found in any particular copy is random. The second setting has forty-two lines throughout, but it is a peculiarity of the original '42-line Bible' that it started out with only forty lines in each column, increased after a few pages to forty-one lines (on one page only) and then finally to the canonical forty-two (compare the opening of Volume I in the Keio University copy and George III's copy in the British Library, Figs 12-13). To accomplish this increased number of lines within the same column measure, the type was at first

Overleaf

12
The opening of the Keio University copy, illuminated in Mainz. St Jerome's Prologue to the Bible, showing the first type-setting of the text and headings printed in red

13
The opening of the British Library paper copy, with Erfurt illumination, in the second type-setting with headings added by hand in red ink

Incipit epistola sancti iheronimi ad
paulinum presbiterum de omnibus
diuine hystorie libris·capitulm pmm.

Rater ambrosius
tua michi munus-
cula pferens·detulit
simul et suauissimas
litas·q a principio
amicicias·fide pba-
te iam fidei et veteris amicicie noua:
pferebant. Vera eni illa necessitudo e-
et xpi glutino copulata·qua non vtili-
tas rei familiaris·no pnia tantum
corpor·no sbdola et palpans adulacio-
sed dei timor· et diuinarum scripturarum
studia conciliant. Legimus in veteribus
hystorijs·quosdam lustrasse puincias a-
nouos adijsse pplos·maria transisse·
ut eos quos ex libris nouerant: cora
qq viderent. Sicut pitagoras mephi-
ticos vates·sic plato egiptu· et archita
tarentinu·eandemq oram ytalie·que
quondam magna grecia dicebat·labo-
riosissime peragrauit· et ut qui athenis
mgr erat· et potens·cuiusq doctrinas
achademie gignasia psonabant·fieret
peginus atq discipulus·malens aliena
verecunde discere: qua sua inpudenter ingerer.
Deniq cum litas quasi toto orbe fugientes psequitur·captus a piratis et venunda-
tus·tyranno crudelissimo paruit·duct9
captiuus vinct9 et seruus. Tamen quia
pfius maior emente se fuit· ad ti tum
liuiu·lacteo eloquentie fonte manantem·
de ultimis hispanie galliarumq finibus
quosdam venisse nobiles legimus· et
quos ad contemplationem sui roma non
traxerat·unus hominis fama perduxit. Habuit illa etas inauditum omnibus seculis·
celebrandumq miraculum·ut urbe tanta

ingressi: aliud extra urbem quererent.
Apolloni9 siue ille mag9·ut uulgus
loquitur·siue phus·ut pitagorici tra-
dunt·intrauit psas·pfiuit caucasum·
albanos·scithas·massagetas·opulen-
tissima indie regna penetrauit· et ad
extremum latissimo physon amne
transmisso puenit ad bragmanas·ut
hyarcam in throno sedente aureo et de
tantali fonte potantem·inter paucos
discipulos·de natura· et de moribus·ac de
cursu dierum et siderum audiret docentem.
Inde per elamitas·babilonios·chalde-
os·medos·assyrios·parthos·syros·
phenices·arabes·palestinos·reuisus
ad allexandriam·perrexit ad ethiopia-
ut gignosophistas et famosissimam
solis mensam uideret in sabulo. Inuenit ille uir ubiqꝫ qd disceret· et semp
proficiens·semp se melior fieret. Scripsit super hoc plenissime octo volumi-
nibus·philostratus.

Quid loquar de seculi hominibus·
cum apostolus paulus·vas electio-
et magister gentiu·qui de conscientia
tanti in se hospitis loquebatur·dicens·An
experimentum queritis eius qui in me
loquitur xpc. Post damasci arabiaq;
lustratam: ascendit iherosolimam ut uideret
petrum et mansit apud eum diebus quindecim.
Hoc eni misterio ebdomadis et ogdo-
adis·futur9 gentiu pdicator instruendus erat. Rursusq post annos quatuordecim assumpto barnaba et tyto: exposuit cum apostolis euangelium·ne forte in vacuum curreret aut cucurrisset. Habet
nescio qd latentis energie·uiue uocis
actus· et in aures discipuli de auctoris
ore transfusa:fortius sonat. Unde et
eschinus cum rodi exularet· et legeretur

Incipit epla sci iheronimi p̄bri ad Pauli
nū p̄sbiterū· de oib̄ diuine hist
orie libris· Capitulū Primū :~

Frater ambrosius
tua michi munuscu
la pferens· detulit
simul ⁊ suauissimas
litteras : que a prin
cipio amiciciaʒ fide
probate iam fidei et veteris amicicie
pferebant. Vera eni illa necessitudo ē
et xp̄i glutino copulata : quā nō vtili
tas rei familiaris· nō p̄ntia tantū
corpo̅·nō subdola ⁊ palpans adulacio:
sed dei timo̅· et diuinarū scripturarū
studia conciliant. Legim̄ in veterib̄
histori s : quosdā lustrasse puincias:
nouos adisse ppl̄os· maria trāsisse:
ut eos quos ex libris nouerāt : corā
q̄ viderent. Sic pitagoras memphi
ticos vates· sic plato egiptū ⁊ archi
tam tarentinū : eamq̄ orā ytalie·que
quondā magna grecia dicebat : labo
riosissime peragrauit : et vt qui athenis
m̄ger erat ⁊ potens· cuiusq̄ doctrinas
achademie gignasia psonabat : fieret
peregrinus atq̄ discipulus : malens a
liena verecude discere : cp̄ sua impu
denter ingerere. Deniq̄ cum litteras
quasi toto orbe fugientes p̄sequitur:
captus a piratis et venudatus· tyran
no crudelissimo paruit - ductus capti
uus vinct̄ et seruus : tamen quia phi
losophus : maior emente se fuit· ad p̄
tumliuiū - lacteo eloquentie fonte ma
nantem de vltimis hispanie galliarū
q̄ finibus quosdam venisse nobiles
legimus : et quos ad cotemplacōnē
sui roma non traxerat : vnius homi
nis fama p̄duxit. Habuit illa etas
inauditum omnibus seculis· celebra
duq̄ miraculū : ut vrbem tantā

ingressi : aliud extra vrbem quererent.
Appolloni̅ siue ille maḡ ut vulgus
loquitur· siue ph̄us ut pitagorici tra
dunt - itrauit psas· ptasiuit caucasū
albanos· scithas· massagetas· opu
lentissima idie regna penetrauit : et
ad extremum latissimo physon amne
trāsmisso puenit ad bragmanas : ut
hyarcam in throno sedente aureo ⁊ de
tantali fonte potantem - inter paucos
discipulos - de natura· de morib̄ ac de
cursu dieru ⁊ sideru audiret docentem.
Inde p elamitas· babilonios· chalde
os - medos - assirios· parthos· syros-
phenices· arabes· palestinos· reuer
sus ad alexandriā - p̄exit ad ethio
piam : ut gignosophistas ⁊ famosissi
mam solis mensam videret i sabulo.
Inuenit ille vir vbiq̄ : quod disceret: ⁊
semp proficiens· semper se melior fie
ret· Scripsit super hoc plenissime octo
voluminibus : phylostratus· ⁋

Quid loquar de seculi hominib̄:
cum apostolus paulus· vas e
leccionis· et magister gentiū-qui de
conscientia tanti in se hospitis loque
batur· dicens· An experimentum que
ritis eius qui in me loquitur cristus:
post damascum arabiaq̄ lustratam
ascendit iherosolimā ut videret petrū
et māsit apud eum diebus quindeci
Hoc eni misterio ebdomadis et og
doadis : futur̄ gentiū p̄dicator
instruendus erat· Rursum post an
nos quatuordecim assumpto barna
ba et tyto - exposuit cum apostolis eu
angelium : ne forte in vacuum curreret
aut cucurrisset· Habet nescio quid la
tentis energie viue vocis actus : et in
aures discipuli de auctoris ore trans
fusa : fortius sonat· Unde et eschines cū
rodi exularet· et legeret illa demostenis

carefully filed down so as to fit more closely, and later recast on a smaller body as the filed types became worn and were discarded. The object of all this effort seems to have been to save on paper and vellum, always a large element of expense. At the beginning of quires with the original 40-line setting, an experiment was made in printing the headings of the chapters in red, as authorized by manuscript tradition; but this was soon abandoned, apparently as being too cumbersome, and a separately printed list of the chapter headings, or rubrics, was instead supplied as a guide for insertion by hand (the process known as rubrication). The rubricator's guides were usually thrown away once they had served their purpose and only two copies, in Munich and Vienna, are known today.

Identification of pre-increase and post-increase pages by their type-setting, paper stocks and ink characteristics has enabled scholars to estimate with a fair claim to precision the original size of the edition and its subsequent revision upwards. The overall increase in the print-run can be calculated at 36 per cent, though the expensive vellum copies were increased proportionately more than the paper ones. If the reasonable assumption is made that the same three to one ratio of paper to vellum Bibles obtained then as it does in extant copies today, we can reckon on a total print-run of about 135 paper copies and about 45 copies on vellum, in accordance

with the high figure of 180 given by Aeneas Sylvius. His lower figure of 158 may reflect with some distortion the situation as it stood before the increase took place. Further scientific analysis of the ink and the paper can show the sequence in which the Bible was set up, but unfortunately the evidence does not permit sure deductions as to the number of presses at work. On the earliest presses, until the beginning of the 1470s, only one page of type could be impressed at a time. As each sheet of paper had in consequence to go under the press four times (two pages on the front of each sheet and two on the back, and a fifth time for the few pages with red-printed chapter headings), an increase in the number of presses must have commended itself early on.

By the beginning of 1455, then, Gutenberg and Fust were in possession of the better part of two hundred large Latin Bibles. At this stage, the books would have been available as loose sheets, four pages on each, each page made of two columns of print. The type-page, that is, the total area covered by print, measures 292 x 198 mm, imposed on a leaf-size of about 430 x 310 mm, though the dimensions of the paper or vellum have usually been much reduced in binding. The sheets would be purchased, despatched and often finished by hand to the owner's taste — rubricated, illuminated, sometimes foliated by addition of leaf numbers — before being bound,

again locally and at the owner's expense. As Aeneas Sylvius's report indicates, the new owners of these first printed books could enjoy a clear and neat 'script' — at least it was clear to fifteenth-century eyes, even if ours have lost the knack of easily unravelling the frequently dense abbreviation. The materials and presswork of the Gutenberg Bible are of famously high quality: the columns are aligned to an even margin (hyphens were allowed to overhang), the words within the columns are evenly spaced out by constant adjustment of abbreviations, the type impressions are crisp, the ink with its high metallic content is very black and glossy, the paper, imported from Italy, is strong and white. A quarter of the extant copies are printed on vellum and these copies (as we know from later custom) would have cost about three times as much as a paper copy, in the belief, not necessarily well founded, that the traditional manuscript material made of animal skins was more robust and lasted longer.

The market for these Bibles was clear: it rarely embraced individuals and only one extant copy, in Vienna, was certainly in private hands in the fifteenth century. But we at least know of churchmen such as Juan de Carvajal and the vicar of St Stephen's in Mainz who owned or wanted to own copies. The Mainz priest was Heinrich Cremer, who is the first person known to have rubricated — as well as illuminating and

binding — a printed book, conveniently dating his notices in both volumes of the Bibliothèque Nationale copy in August 1456 (Fig. 4). Cremer's work of hand-finishing the printed volume (a feature of book production that continued for decades) may have been done on behalf of the archbishop of Mainz.

But Gutenberg and Fust could expect to sell more especially to the reformed monasteries which were dotted all over Germany, particularly in the south. We have to imagine a tremendous marketing campaign which took the sellers on horseback around the German-speaking lands with samples of their wares to show to abbots and priors and superiors — the loose quires that were seen at Frankfurt in 1454 will have been part of the effort. However it was done, Aeneas Sylvius is witness to the extraordinary fact that the book was sold out in advance of publication. Benedictine, Cistercian and Carthusian monks, Augustinians, Franciscan and Carmelite friars, Brigittine nuns and Sisters of the Common Life, are all known to have owned copies of the Gutenberg Bible in the fifteenth century. There is evidence too of early sales even outside Germany and Austria, certainly to the Netherlands and even to England. The edition offered the standard version of the Latin text made at the University of Paris in the thirteenth century. Innovation in this area would not have

been welcome, might indeed have proved fatal to the venture. A key to the success of the marketing exercise was the underlying movement towards standardization of texts, in the first place for uniformity of divine service; but of course the huge advantages of uniformity in other sorts of writing, in terms of textual authority and ease of reference, soon became apparent to users and producers of printed books. These Bibles may well have been designed for the communal readings which were a feature of contemporary monastic life. More than one copy still bears the markings for reading in the monastic refectory. Others may have been placed on the high altar of churches, for display rather than use.

After the fitful light shed by the two documents of 1455 — the letter of Aeneas Sylvius and the Helmasperger Instrument — darkness again descends on the activities of Johann Gutenberg. A reasonable estimate of the likely profit on the sale of 180 Bibles is very difficult to arrive at since practically all the quantities are unknown. The only recorded price is the 100 Rhenish guilders paid for the vellum copy now in the Huntington Library in California, but that very likely included the binding and extensive illumination, both in this case carried out at Leipzig (Fig. 14; the same illuminator was responsible for the splendid decoration of the Berlin copy, Fig. 15). An unbound paper copy without illumination might have

fetched a more affordable 20 guilders, perhaps a third or a quarter of the price of a good manuscript of the Bible. Those who have attempted to work out a scheme of outgoings, turnover and profit have come to the conclusion that Gutenberg should easily have recouped his expenses and been in a position to repay Fust his loan with all the accumulated interest. Yet at the end of 1455, just when there should have been a large influx of funds from sales of the books, Fust obtained a court order against Gutenberg and appears to have put him out of business by having his equipment confiscated. No doubt returns on the sale of the Bible were slow to come, and we have to suppose that many remained unpaid for by the time of the judgement recorded in the Helmasperger Instrument. It is better to admit frankly that without new evidence, which is unlikely now to be forthcoming, we shall never be able to divine the circumstances of Gutenberg's downfall.

For downfall is what it seems to have been. Fust himself continued in business, printing in a new partnership with the craftsman Peter Schöffer, formerly the assistant of Gutenberg and one of the witnesses on Fust's side in the court case. Together they produced a whole series of monumental editions which they signed and dated from 1457 onwards, notably the beautiful Psalter of that year, in the design of

Overleaf

14
The vellum copy in the Huntington Library, California, bound and illuminated at Leipzig

15
The Staatsbibliothek zu Berlin paper copy, illuminated in the same Leipzig workshop as the Huntington Bible

ncipit liber bresith que[m] nos genesim dicim[us]. In principio creauit deus celu[m] et terram. Terra aute[m] erat inanis et vacua: et tenebre erant sup[er] faciem abissi: et sp[iritu]s d[omi]ni ferebat[ur] sup[er] aquas. Dixit[que] deus. Fiat lux. Et facta e[st] lux. Et vidit deus luce[m] q[uod] esset bona: et diuisit luce[m] a tenebris: appellauit[que] luce[m] die[m] et tenebras nocte[m]. Factu[m]q[ue] e[st] vespe[re] et mane dies vnus. Dixit q[uo]q[ue] deus. Fiat firmamentu[m] in medio aquar[um]: et diuidat aquas ab aquis. Et fecit deus firmamentu[m]: diuisitq[ue] aquas que erat sub firmamento ab hiis q[ue] erant sup[er] firmamentu[m]: et factu[m] e[st] ita. Vocauit[que] deus firmamentu[m] celu[m]: et factu[m] e[st] vespe[re] et mane dies sec[un]d[us]. Dixit vero deus. Cong[re]gent[ur] aque que sub celo su[n]t in locu[m] vnu[m] et appareat arida. Et factu[m] e[st] ita. Et vocauit deus aridam terram: cong[re]gacionesq[ue] aquar[um] appellauit maria. Et vidit deus q[uod] esset bonu[m]: et ait. Germinet terra herba[m] virente[m] et facie[n]te[m] seme[n]: et lignu[m] pomifer[um] faciens fructu[m] iuxta genus suu[m]: cui[us] seme[n] in semetipso sit sup[er] terra[m]. Et factu[m] e[st] ita. Et p[ro]tulit terra herba[m] virente[m] et facie[n]te[m] se[m]e[n] iuxta genus suu[m]: lignu[m]q[ue] faciens fructu[m] et habens vnu[m]q[uo]dq[ue] seme[n]te[m] sec[un]d[um] specie[m] sua[m]. Et vidit deus q[uod] esset bonu[m]: et factu[m] e[st] vespe[re] et mane dies tercius. Dixit[que] aute[m] deus. Fiant luminaria in firmame[n]to celi: et diuidant die[m] ac nocte[m]: et sint in signa et t[em]pa et dies et annos: vt luceant in firmame[n]to celi et illumine[n]t terra[m]. Et factu[m] e[st] ita. Fecitq[ue] deus duo luminaria magna: lumi[n]are maius vt p[re]esset diei et luminare min[us] vt p[re]esset nocti et stellas: et posuit eas in firmame[n]to celi vt lucere[n]t sup[er] terra[m]: et

p[re]essent diei ac nocti: et diuiderent luce[m] ac tenebras. Et vidit de[us] q[uod] esset bonu[m]: et factu[m] e[st] vespe[re] et mane dies quart[us]. Dixit etia[m] de[us]. Producant aque reptile anime viue[n]tis et volatile sup[er] terra[m] sub firmame[n]to celi. Creauitq[ue] deus cete grandia et omne[m] a[n]i[m]a[m] viue[n]te[m] atq[ue] motabile[m] qua[m] p[ro]duxerat aque i[n] species suas: et omne volatile sec[un]d[um] gen[us] suu[m]. Et vidit deus q[uod] esset bonu[m]: benedixitq[ue] eis dicens. Crescite et multiplicamini et replete aquas maris: auesq[ue] multiplice[n]t[ur] sup[er] terra[m]. Et factu[m] e[st] vespe[re] et mane dies quint[us]. Dixit q[uo]q[ue] deus. Producat terra a[n]i[m]a[m] viue[n]te[m] in gene[re] suo: iume[n]ta et reptilia et bestias terre sec[un]d[um] species suas. Factu[m]q[ue] e[st] ita. Et fecit de[us] bestias terre iuxta species suas: et iume[n]ta et omne reptile terre i[n] genere suo. Et vidit deus q[uod] esset bonu[m]: et ait. Facia[mus] hoie[m] ad ymagine[m] et similitudine[m] nostra[m]: et p[re]sit piscib[us] maris et volatilib[us] celi et bestiis vniuerseq[ue] terre: omniq[ue] reptili q[uo]d mouet[ur] i[n] terra. Et creauit deus hoie[m] ad ymagine[m] et similitudine[m] sua[m]: ad ymagine[m] d[e]i creauit illu[m]: masculu[m] et femina[m] creauit eos. Benedixitq[ue] illis deus et ait. Crescite et multiplicamini et replete terra[m]: et subicite ea[m]: et d[omi]namini piscib[us] maris et volatilib[us] celi et vniuersis a[n]ima[n]tib[us] que mouent[ur] sup[er] terra[m]. Dixitq[ue] de[us]. Ecce dedi vobis omne[m] herba[m] affere[n]te[m] seme[n] sup[er] terra[m] et vniu[er]sa ligna que h[abe]nt i[n] semetipis seme[n]te[m] gene[r]is sui: vt sint vobis i[n] esca[m] et cu[n]ctis a[n]ima[n]tib[us] terre: omniq[ue] volucri celi et vniuersis q[ue] mouent[ur] i[n] terra et i[n] quib[us] est a[n]i[m]a viue[n]s: vt h[abe]a[n]t ad vescendu[m]. Et factu[m] e[st] ita. Vidit[que] deus cu[n]cta que fecerat: et erant valde bona.

Incipit liber bresith quem nos genesim dicimus. In principio creauit deus celum et terram. Terra autem erat inanis et uacua: et tenebre erant sup facie abissi: et sps dni ferebat sup aquas. Dixitq; deus. Fiat lux. Et facta e lux. Et vidit deus lucem qp esset bona: et diuisit luce a tenebris appellauitq; lucem diem et tenebras noctem. Factumq; est vespe et mane dies unus. Dixit qp deus. Fiat firmamentu in medio aquaru: et diuidat aquas ab aquis. Et fecit deus firmamentu: diuisitq; aquas que erant sub firmamento ab hijs q erant sup firmamentu: et factu e ita. Vocauitq; deus firmamentu celu: et factu e vespe et mane dies sedcs. Dixit vero deus. Congregent aque que sub celo sunt in locu unu et appareat arida. Et factu e ita. Et vocauit deus aridam terram: congregacionesq; aquaru appellauit maria. Et vidit deus qp esset bonu: et ait. Germinet terra herbam virentem et facientem semen: et lignu pomiferu faciens fructu iuxta genus suu: cui9 semen in semetipso sit sup terra. Et factu e ita. Et protulit terra herbam virentem et facientem semen iuxta genus suu: lignuq; faciens fructu et habens unuqdq; semente sedm speciem sua. Et vidit deus qp esset bonu: et factu e vespe et mane dies tercius. Dixitq; aute deus. Fiant luminaria in firmameto celi et diuidant diem ac noctem: et sint in signa et tpa et dies et annos: ut luceant in firmameto celi et illuminent terra. Et factu e ita. Fecitq; deus duo luminaria magna: luminare maius ut pesset diei et luminare min9 ut pesset nocti et stellas et posuit eas in firmameto celi ut lucerent sup terra: et

presserent diei ac nocti: et diuiderent luce ac tenebras. Et vidit de9 qp esset bonu: et factu e vespe et mane dies quartus. Dixit etia de9. Producat aque reptile anime viuentis et volatile super terra sub firmameto celi. Creauitq; deus cete grandia: et omne aiam viuente atq; morabile qua pduxerat aque i specie suas: et omne volatile sedm gen9 suu. Et vidit deus qp esset bonu: benedixitq; eis dicens. Crescite et multiplicamini: et replete aquas maris: auesq; multiplicent sup terra. Et factu e vespe et mane dies quintus. Dixit quoq; deus. Producat terra aiam viuente in gene suo: iumenta et reptilia: et bestias terre sedm species suas. Factuq; ita. Et fecit de9 bestias terre iuxta species suas: iumenta et omne reptile terre i genere suo. Et vidit deus qp esset bonu: et ait. Faciamus hoiem ad ymagine et similitudine nostra: et psit piscibus maris: et volatilibus celi: et bestijs uniuerseq; terre: omniq; reptili qd mouetur i terra. Et creauit deus hoiem ad ymagine et similitudine sua: ad ymagine dei creauit illu: masculu et femina creauit eos. Benedixitq; illis deus: et ait. Crescite et multiplicamini: et replete terra: et sbicite eam et dominamini piscibus maris: et volatilibus celi: et uniuersis animatibus que mouetur sup terra. Dixitq; de9. Ecce dedi vobis omne herba afferente semen sup terra: et uniuersa ligna que hut in semetipsis semente genis sui: ut sint vobis i escam: et cunctis aiantibus terre: omniq; volucri celi: et uniuersis q mouentur in terra: i quibus est anima viuens: ut habeat ad vescendu. Et factu est ita. Vidit deus cuncta que fecerat: et erant valde bona.

Dñicis diebz poſt feſtũ tꝛinitatis · Inuitatoꝛiũ.

Rege magnũ dñm venite adoꝛemus, ꝑs Venite.
Dñicis diebz poſt feſtũ ephie Inuitatoꝛiũ.

Adoꝛem⁹ dñm qui feᵗt nos, Or venite aũ Scrute.

Eatus vir qui non abijt in conſilio impioꝛũ et in via pᶜcoꝛ nõ ſtetit: ⁊ in cathedra peſtilēcie nõ ſedit. Sed ĩ lege dñi voluntas ei⁹: et in lege eius meditabiᵗt die ac nocte, Et erit tanꝗ lignũ qð plātatũ iſt ſecus decurſus aꝗe: qð frucꝛu ſuũ dabit in ꝑꝛ ſuo Et foliũ ei⁹ nõ deffluet: ⁊ oĩa qᶜũꝗ faciet pſpᶜrabũᵗt, Nõ ſic impij nõ ſic ſed tanꝗ puluis quē ꝓicit vᶜntus a facie terre, Ideo non reſurgᵗt impij in iudicio: neꝗ pᶜcoꝛes in cõſilio iuſtoꝛ Qm nouit dñs viã iuſtoꝛ: ⁊ iter impioꝛ ꝑribit, O ha ꝑ

whose type Gutenberg surely had a hand (Fig. 16). But Gutenberg cannot definitely be assigned any piece of printing after the Bible, and traces of him after 1455 are very scant. In 1457 he defaulted for the first time on the annual interest payment of a debt contracted many years before at Strassburg, which suggests that his finances were in poor shape. A mysterious and now controversial book, the large Latin dictionary called *Catholicon*, was printed in a new, smaller type in 1460 and subsequently, but it is not clear whether Gutenberg was responsible for it.

Two last documents mention Gutenberg by name. In 1465 he was granted a pension by the Archbishop of Mainz, Adolf of Nassau, whose violent assault upon the city three years before had led to a great dispersal of many citizens and tradesmen, including printers. Gutenberg had probably been among them, but he was now admitted as the archbishop's courtier and servant for undisclosed 'agreeable and willing services'; the pension included specified quantities of grain and wine — about 2,000 litres annually — as well as tax exemptions. Whether these services included organization of a printing establishment at Mainz or at the archbishop's seat at nearby Eltville is once again a matter of speculation. But it is not doubted that Gutenberg retained a live interest in the art he had brought into being, for on 26 February 1468 one

Dr Konrad Homery, a leading Mainz lawyer, formally acknowledged receipt of printing equipment left at Gutenberg's death, though it was Homery's own property. Dr Homery was plainly in some sense Gutenberg's patron in his last years but we cannot point to anything produced under this patronage, unless indeed it was the *Catholicon*. According to an obituary notice of uncertain authenticity written in a book which was printed some years after Gutenberg's death and is now lost, the inventor died on 3 February 1468. He was buried in the church of the Mainz Franciscans. All trace of his grave was lost in successive rebuildings of the church and its ultimate destruction in 1793.

Gutenberg's true monument is the forty-eight surviving copies of the Bible, about twenty of them complete. Some of them consist of a single volume or less, a quarter of the total are printed on vellum. By the standards of fifteenth-century printing, the Gutenberg Bible is not now an uncommon book: the 36-line Bible, for example, printed by the successor to Gutenberg's types, is very much rarer. But for centuries no other book has been so sought after or brought such cachet to the collections where copies are housed. A complete 42-line Bible is usually divided after the Psalms of the Old Testament, thus making two large folio volumes of 324 and 319 leaves. Vellum copies, being very much heavier than

paper, are often bound in three or even four volumes. As in contemporary manuscripts, each book of the Bible has a preface by St Jerome, the translator of the Latin Vulgate from the original Hebrew and Greek. These prologues, and the following biblical texts, are commonly adorned with elaborate initials added by hand, and many copies have more extensive illumination in burnished gold and colours painted by artists at the major divisions of the text.

Much of the current interest in the Bible lies in determining the original owners or provenance of the extant copies, nearly all of which are now in the large public libraries of Western Europe and the United States (two which were housed in Leipzig until the end of the Second World War have recently surfaced in Russia, and a single volume was acquired in 1996 by Keio University in Tokyo). The identification of provenance, which as well as having its own fascination is our best guide to the original market, depends on evidence of several kinds: inscriptions, style of illumination and of rubrication, and (in the rare cases where they survive) original bindings.

Art historians can identify with increasing accuracy the likely place of origin of specific styles of painting, in some cases following the lead of historians of bookbinding. The Keio University copy, for example, is in a binding which is

Epla sci ieronimi pbri ad chromaciu
et eliodoꝝ epos de libris salomonis
iungat epistola quos iungit sacerdo-
tium: immo carta non diuidat: quos
xpi nectit amor. Comentarios in ose-
am: amos: z zachariam: malachiam quoq;
poscitis. Scripsissem: si licuisset pꝛ uali-
tudine. Mittitis solacia sumptuum:
notarios nꝝos et librarios sustentatis: ut uobis potissimum nꝝm desude-
tingeniu. Et ecce ex latere freques turba
diuersa poscentiu: quasi aut equu sit me
uobis esurientibus alijs laborare: aut
in racione dati et accepti: cuiusq; preter
uos obnoxius sim. Ataq; longa egrota-
cione fractus: ne penitus hoc anno reticerem: z apud uos mutus essem: tridui opus nomini uestro consecraui: interp-
tacionem videlicet triu salomonis uo-
luminu: masloth qd hebrei pabolas:
uulgata editio ꝑubia uocat: coeleth
que grece ecclesiasten latine cocionatore
possum dicere: siraciim: qd i lingua
nꝝam uertit canticu cancoꝛu. Fertur et
panaretos: ihu filij sirach liber: z alij
pseudographus: qui sapientia salomonis inscribit. Quoꝝ priore hebraicum reperi: non ecclesiasticu ut apud latinos: sed pabolas ꝑnotatu. Cui iuct
erant ecclesiastes et canticu canticoꝛ: ut
similitudine salomonis non solum numero libroꝝ: sed etia materiaꝝ genere coequaret. Secudus apud hebreos
nusq; est: quia et ipse stilus grecam
eloquenciam redolet: et nonulli scriptoꝛ
veteꝛ hunc esse iudei filonis affirmant.
Sicut ergo iudith z thobie z macha-
beoꝝ libros: legit quide eos ecclia: sed
inter canonicas scripturas non recipit:
sic z hec duo uolumina legat ad edi-
ficatione plebis: non ad auctoritatem
ecclesiasticoꝝ dogmatu afirmandam.

Si cui sane septuaginta interpretum
magis editio placet: habet eam a nobis
olim emedatam. Neq; enim noua sic cu-
dim: ut uetera destruam. Et tame cu
diligentissime legerit: sciat magis nꝝa
scripta intelligi: que non in tertium uas
transfusa coacuerit: sed statim de preto
purissime comedata testei: suum sapore ser-
uauerit. Explicit epla Incipit libⸯ puloꝛ—

Parabole salomonis   A
filij dauid regis israel:
ad sciendam sapienti-
am z disciplinam: ad
intelligenda verba
prudentie et suscipi-
endam eruditione doctrine: iusticia
et iudiciu z equitate: ut detur paruulis
astucia: et adolescenti sciencia et intellectus. Audies sapiens sapiencior erit: z
intelliges gubernacla possidebit. Ani-
aduertet parabolam et interpretacio-
nem: verba sapientiu z enigmata eoꝝ.
Timor dni pricipiu sapiencie. Sapien-
ciam atq; doctrinam stulti despiciut.
Audi fili mi disciplinam pris tui et ne
dimittas legem mris tue: ut addetur
gratia capiti tuo: z torques collo tuo.
Fili mi si te lactauerint peccatores: ne acquiescas eis. Si dixerint veni nobiscu-
insidiemur saguini: abscodam edi   B
culas cotra insontem frustra: degluta-
mus eu sicut infernus viuente z integrum quasi descendente in lacu: omne
preciosa substancia repperiem: imple-
bim domus nꝝas spolijs: sortem mitte nobiscum: marsupiu sit unum omniu
nꝝm: fili mi ne ambules cu eis. Prohibe pedem tuu a semitis eoꝝ. Pedes
eni illoꝝ ad malu curruut: z festinant ut
effundant saguinem. Frustra autem
iacit rete ante oculos pennatoꝝ. Ipi ꝗ-
coutra sanguine suu insidiantur: et

identifiably Mainz work, and since these operations were generally carried out in close succession, the charming floral decoration of the opening page is attributed to Mainz also (Fig. 12). A different Mainz illuminator is seen at work in copies in Burgos in Spain (Fig. 17) and in the Pierpont Morgan Library in New York. From continued association with the products of Gutenberg, Fust and Schöffer, this expert artist has been christened the Fust Master: it is supposed that he was a sort of in-house illuminator for the early Mainz press. A copy in Eton College Library which belonged to the Erfurt Carthusians was also illuminated there, and handsomely bound by a local binder, Johannes Fogel, who inscribed his name on the binding (Fig. 18). Three more of the existing ten original bindings are in a very similar style and have been associated with him. One of those is the Bible in the Scheide collection in Princeton, which is otherwise notable for its illumination: the animal motifs of this copy are closely copied from designs engraved on playing cards which were widespread in Germany in the years before the printing of the Bible (Figs 19-21).

Erfurt, an ecclesiastical centre some 150 miles from Mainz, seems indeed to have taken a large part in the illumination and binding of copies of the Bible. No fewer than six are thought to have been decorated there, including one now

17
*A copy
illuminated by
the 'Fust
Master' in
Mainz
(Burgos,
Biblioteca
Pública,
opening page
of the second
volume)*

in the National Library of Scotland (Fig. 22). Another is the paper copy from the library of King George III, now in the British Library, which also owns a complete but undecorated vellum copy formerly belonging to the Mainz Carthusians. The paper copy has fine illumination at the chief divisions of the book, that is, at the prologues which begin each volume and at the opening of Genesis, on the ninth page of the first volume. The pages show elaborate oversized initials with borders of riotous foliage on which are perched a variety of exotic birds and animals (Figs 12, 23-24). The initials, here and elsewhere, sometimes incorporate small figures (Fig. 23, God the Father, and Fig. 25, Solomon proclaiming his proverbs). The King's Library copy followed a path to England which, by coincidence, was likewise followed in the eighteenth century by a 36-line Bible. Both came from the Schottenkloster, or monastery of the Irish Benedictines, in Würzburg, about 80 miles up the river Main from Mainz. It is a pleasant thought that Johann Trithemius, one of the founding fathers of bibliography and abbot of the Schottenkloster from 1506, could have overseen refectory readings from both these great monuments of early printing.

A last specimen gives a small and quite unexpected clue to the early reach of the printing press. Recently retrieved from an old collection of fragments in the British Library is a

18
The Eton
College Bible
has a
contemporary
binding signed
by the Erfurt
binder
Johannes Fogel

19-21

*Details of the Scheide Bible (Princeton, New Jersey), with Erfurt illumination
based on contemporary playing-card designs.*

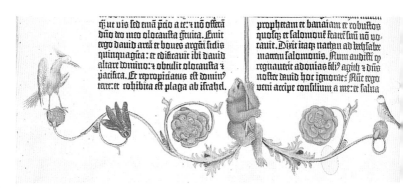

single illuminated vellum leaf. The illumination is decidedly English in style and undoubtedly dates from the fifteenth century (Fig. 26). The discovery at first prompted thoughts that the leaf came from the volume of the Bible which is preserved at Lambeth Palace, the seat of the Archbishop of Canterbury in London (this copy was long thought to be a manuscript, so close was Gutenberg's type to the appearance of contemporary handwriting). The Lambeth vellum New Testament, however, turned out to have the same leaf quite intact

and illuminated in exactly the same style (Fig. 27). This can only indicate the very remarkable fact that at least two Gutenberg Bibles — expensive vellum copies at that — made their way over the North Sea to some workshop in London at a very early stage: these were the first printed books ever seen in England.

This single leaf now displayed in the British Library galleries, battered and rather shabby as it is, presages the worldwide revolution that was to overtake the ownership and distribution of books thanks to Gutenberg's invention. And ownership of and access to printed texts of all sorts has been incomparably the most significant factor in human intellectual progress over the last five centuries. We are now witnessing the early stages of a new revolution in the transmission of information, but the book as we know it, Gutenberg's great legacy to Western civilization, will be with us for some time to come.

Incipit prologus sancti ieronimi
presbiteri in parabolas salomonis
iungat epistola quos iungit sacerdoti
um: immo carta non diuidat: quos
xpi nectit amor. Commetarios in osee.
amos. z zachariam malachiam . quoqz
poscitis. Scripsisse: si licuisset pre uali-
tudine. Mittitis solacia sumptuum.
notarios nostros et librarios sustentatis: ut uobis potissimu nostrum desudet
ingeniu. Et ecce ex latere frequens turba
diuisa poscetiu: quasi aut equum sit me
uobis esurientibz alijs laborare: aut
in racione dati et accepti. cuiqz preter
uos obnoxi9 sim. Itaqz longa egrotatione fractus. ne penitus hoc anno re-
ticere. z apud uos mutus essem. tridui
opus nomini uestro consecraui. interp-
tatione uidelicet triu salomonis uo-
luminu: masloth qd hebrei parabolas.
uulgata editio puibia uocat: coeleth.
que grece eccliasten. latine ocionatore
possum9 dicere: sirasirim. qd i lingua
nostram uertit canticu canticor. Fertur et
panaretos. ihu filij sirach liber: z ali9
pseudographus. qui sapientia salomonis inscribit. Quor priore hebraicum repperi. non eccliasticum apud latinos: sed parabolas pnotatum. Cui

23

The end of St Jerome's Prologue and beginning of the Book of Genesis, with Erfurt illumination (British Library C.9.d.3)

pnouocauit:qui editioni ãtique tãsla=
tione theodotionis miscuit:asterico et
obelo id est stella et veru omne opus
distinguens:dum aut illucescere facit
que minus ante fuerãt:aut supflua
queq̃ iugulat et cõfodit: et maxime
que euangelistarũ et apostolorũ auc=
toritas promulgauit. In quibus mul=
ta de veteri testamento legimus que i
nostris codicibus non habentur: ut
est illud·ex egypto vocaui filiũ meũ: et
quonia nazarenus vocabitur: et vi=
debunt in quẽ cõpunxerũt:et flumina
de ventre eius fluent aque viue: et que
nec oculus vidit nec auris audiuit nec
in cor hominis ascendit que prepara=
uit diligentibus se: et multa alia que
propriũ sintagma desiderant. Inter=
rogemus ergo eos ubi hec scripta sint:
et cum dicere non potuerint·de libris
hebraicis proferam·Primũ testimo=
niũ est in osee·secundũ in esaia·terciũ
i zacharia·quartũ in puerbiis·quintũ
eque in esaia: qñ multi ignorãtes ap=
crifo speliramentã sectant: et hibereas ne=
nias libris autenticis pferũt. Causas
erroris nõ est meũ exponere. Iudei pru=
denti factũ dicũt esse cõsilio: ne ptolo=
meus unius dei cultor etiã apud hebreos
duplicẽ diuinitatẽ cõprehederet: qñ
maxime idcirco faciebat quia in pla=
tonis dogma cadere videbat. Deniq̃·
ubicumq̃ sacratũ aliqd scriptura testat
de pãtre filio et spiritu sãcto aut aliter
interptati sũt aut omnino tacuerũt: ut
et regi satisfacerẽt: et archanũ fidei nõ
vulgarent. Et nescio quis pm᷑ auctor
septuaginta cellulas alexandrie men=
dacio suo extruxerit·quibus diuisi eadẽ
scriptarent: cũ aristeus eiusdẽ ptolo=
mei yperaspistes·et nõ multo post tempore
iosephus nichil tale retulerint: sed in

una basilica congreg[ate]
scribãt non pheta[sse].
vatem: aliud ẽ esse in[ter]
ventura pdicit: hic erud[ita]
copia ea que intelligit
forte putabus est tulli[um]
xenofontis et platonis
mostenis pheseforurã[?]
rico spiritu trãstulisse.
ideũ libris per septua[ginta]
aliter p apostolos spir[itu]
stimonia requir: ut q̃ i[n]
scriptũ esse meniti sint.
Damnam᷑ veteres ? sm[?]
prioũ studia in domi[?]
sumus laborarã·? All[?]
ãte aduentũ xpi et qd v[?]
proultutũ[?] sentencias: n[?]
nem eius non tam pb[?]
am scabim᷑. Aliter en[?]
ter visa narrantur. Qd[?]
mus meli᷑ et proferim᷑
smule: obtrectator aus[?]
mno non reprehendo
sed confidenter tuchis i[?]
pfero. Per istos os ni[?]
quos aute phetas in[?]
carisinata positos lego:[?]
pene gradu intexpres ter[?]
re torqueris ? Quid speta[?]
me ãutas ? Sicubi i tra[?]
dor errare interroga hebr[?]
urbiũ mgros cõsule. N[?]
xpo tui codices nõ habe[?]
cõtra se postea ab aplis[?]
monia pbauerit: et eu[?]
templaria latina·gñ grec[?]
brea. Hẽ bx̃ orta iundo[?]
cor desidri carissime: ut q[?]
sbine fecisti et a genesi expo[?]
nibis inues: qñ posli eõr̃ s[?]
sũt libri i latinũ eos trã[?]

Incipit liber Bresith que[m] nos Gene
sim dicim[us]. In principio creauit deus celu[m] [et]
et terra[m]. Terra autem erat inanis et
vacua:[et] tenebre erant sup[er] facie[m] abissi:
et sp[irit]us d[omi]ni ferebatur sup[er] aquas.
Dixitq[ue] deus. Fiat lux. Et facta e[st] lux.
Et vidit deus luce[m] q[uo]d esset bona:et
diuisit luce[m] a tenebris:appellauitq[ue]
luce[m] die[m] et tenebras noctem. Factu[m]
e[st] [que] vespere [et] mane dies vnus. Dixit
quoq[ue] deus. Fiat firmamentu[m] in me
dio aquar[um]: et diuidat aquas ab a
quis. Et fecit deus firmamentu[m]: diui
sitq[ue] aquas que erant sub firmame[n]
to ab hijs que erant sup[er] firmame[n]
tum:[et] factu[m] est ita. Vocauitq[ue] deus
firmamentu[m] celu[m]:[et] factum est vespere
et mane dies secundus. Dixit vero de
us. Congregent[ur] aque que sub celo
sunt in locum vnu[m] et appareat arida.
Et factu[m] est ita. Et vocauit deus ari
dam terra[m]:congregationesq[ue] aquas
appellauit maria. Et vidit deus q[uod] es
set bonu[m] et ait. Germinet terra herba[m]
virentem et facientem seme[n]: et lignu[m]
pomiferu[m] faciens fructum iuxta genu[s]
suu[m]: cuius seme[n] in semetipso sit sup[er]
terram. Et factum est ita. Et protulit
terra herbam virentem et faciente[m] se
men iuxta genus suu[m]:lignu[m]q[ue] faciens
fructu[m] et habens vnu[m]q[uod]q[ue] seme[n] sec[un]dum
specie[m] sua[m]. Et vidit deus q[uod] esset bonu[m]:
et factu[m] e[st] vespere et mane dies tercius.
Dixitq[ue] aut[em] deus. Fiant luminaria
in firmame[n]to celi:[et] diuidant die[m] ac
nocte[m]:[et] sint in signa [et] te[m]pora:[et] dies [et]
annos:ut luceant in firmame[n]to celi et
illumine[n]t terra[m]. Et factu[m] est ita. Fecitq[ue]
deus duo luminaria magna:lumi[n]are
maius ut p[re]esset diei et luminare min[us]
ut p[re]esset nocti:[et] stellas:[et] p[ro]suit eas i[n]
firmame[n]to celi ut lucere[n]t sup[er] terra[m]: [et]

p[re]essent diei ac nocti:[et] diuiderent luce[m]
ac tenebras. Et vidit de[us] q[uod] esset bonu[m]:
et factu[m] e[st] vespere et mane dies quart[us].
Dixit etiam deus. Producant aque
reptile anime viuentis et volatile sup[er]
terram: sub firmame[n]to celi. Creauitq[ue]
deus cete grandia:et omne anima[m] vi
uentem atq[ue] motabilem qua[m] produxe
rant aque in species suas:[et] omne vo
latile secundu[m] genus suu[m]. Et vidit de
us q[uod] esset bonu[m]: benedixitq[ue] ei dicens.
Crescite et multiplicamini:et replete a
quas maris:auesq[ue] multiplicent[ur]
sup[er] terram. Et factu[m] e[st] vespere [et] mane
dies quintus. Dixit quoq[ue] deus. Pro
ducat terra anima[m] viuente[m] in gene
re suo:iumenta [et] reptilia:[et] bestias ter
re secundu[m] species suas. Factu[m] e[st] ita. Et
fecit deus bestias terre iuxta species su
as:iumenta [et] omne reptile terre in ge
nere suo. Et vidit deus q[uod] esset bonu[m]:
et ait. Faciam[us] homine[m] ad ymagine[m] [et]
similitudine[m] nostra[m]:[et] p[re]sit piscib[us] maris:
[et] volatilib[us] celi:[et] bestijs vniuerseq[ue] terre:
omniq[ue] reptili q[uod] mouet[ur] in terra. Et crea
uit deus homine[m] ad ymagine[m] et simi
litudine[m] suam: ad ymagine[m] dei crea
uit illu[m]:masculu[m] [et] femina[m] creauit eos.
Benedixitq[ue] illis deus:[et] ait. Crescite
et multiplicamini:[et] replete terram:[et]
subijcite eam:[et] dominamini piscib[us]
maris:[et] volatilib[us] celi:[et] vniuersis
animantib[us] que mouentur sup[er] terra[m].
Dixitq[ue] deus. Ecce dedi vobis omne[m]
herbam afferentem seme[n] sup[er] terram:
et vniuersa ligna que habent i[n] semetip[s]is
seme[n]te[m] generis sui:ut sint vobis i[n] esca[m]:
[et] cu[n]ctis a[n]imantib[us] terre:omniq[ue] volucri
celi [et] vniuersis q[ue] mouentur in terra:et i[n]
quibus e[st] anima viue[n]s:ut habeat ad
vescendu[m]. Et factu[m] est ita. Vidit q[ue] deus
cu[n]cta que fecerat:[et] erant valde bona.

Incipit prologus sancti theodori presbiteri in parabolas salomonis

Iungat epistola quos iungit sacerdocium: immo carta non dividat: quos xpi nectit amor. Comentarios in osee. amos. z zachariam malachiam quoque poscitis. Scripsissem: si licuisset pro valitudine. Mittitis solacia sumptuum: notarios nros z librarios sustentatis: ut vobis potissimum nrm desudet ingenium. Et ecce ex latere frequens turba diversa poscentium: quasi aut equum sit me vobis esurientibus aliis laborare: aut in ratione dati et accepti: cuiquam preter vos obnoxius sim. Itaque longa egrotatione fractus: ne penitus hoc anno reticerem: z apud vos mutus essem: triduum opus nomini vro consecravi: interpretatione videlicet trium salomonis voluminum: masloth qd hebrei parabolas vulgata editio pprouerbia vocat: coelethque grece ecclesiasten latine oratorem possum dicere: sirasirim qd i linguam nram vertitur canticum canticorum. Fertur et panaretos iesu filii syrach liber: z alius pseudographus qui sapientia salomonis inscribit. Quorum priorem hebraicum reperi: non ecclesiasticu ut apud latinos: sed parabolas pnotatu. Cui iuncti erant ecclesiastes: et canticu canticorum: ut similitudine salomonis: non solum numero librorum: sed etiam materiar genere coequaret. Secundus apud hebreos nusquam est: quia et ipse stilus grecam eloquentiam redolet: et nonulli scriptorum veteru hunc esse iudei filonis affirmant. Sicut ergo iudith z thobie z machabeor libros: legit quide eos ecclesia: sed inter canonicas scripturas non recipit: sic z hec duo volumina legat ad edificationem plebis: non ad auctoritatem ecclesiasticor dogmatu firmandam.

Si cui sane septuaginta interpretum magis editio placet: habet eam a nobis olim emendatam. Neque enim nova sic cudimus: ut vetera destruamus. Et tamen cum diligentissime legerit: sciat magis nostra scripta intelligi: que non in tertium vas transfusa coacuerint: sed statim de prelo purissimam commendata teste: suum saporem servaverint. Incipiut parabole salomonis

Parabole salomonis filii david regis israel: ad sciendam sapientiam z disciplinam: ad intelligenda verba prudentie et suscipiendam eruditionem doctrine: iustitiam et iudicium z equitatem: ut detur parvulis astutia: et adolescenti scientia et intellectus. Audiens sapiens sapientior erit: z intelliges gubernacula possidebit. Animadvertet parabolam et interpretationem: verba sapientum z enigmata eorum. Timor dni principium sapientie. Sapientiam atque doctrinam stulti despiciunt. Audi fili mi disciplinam pris tui et ne dimittas legem matris tue: ut addatur gratia capiti tuo: z torques collo tuo. Fili mi si te lactaverint peccatores: ne acquiescas eis. Si dixerint veni nobiscum insidiemur sanguini: abscondamus tendiculas contra insontem frustra: degluciamus eum sicut infernus viventem z integrum: quasi descendentem in lacum: omnem preciosam substantiam reperiemus: implebimus domus nostras spoliis: sortem mitte nobiscum: marsupium sit unum omnium nostrum: fili mi ne ambules cum eis. Prohibe pedem tuu a semitis eor. Pedes enim illor ad malum currut: z festinant ut effundant sanguinem. Frustra autem iacitur rete ante oculos pennatorum. Ipsi quoque contra sanguinem suu insidiantur.

Left

24
The opening
page of the
2nd volume
(Parabole or
Proverbs) of
the British
Library paper
copy
(IC.9.d.4)

Right

25
Solomon in
his glory:
detail of Fig.
24

Overleaf

26
The British
Library
fragment of St
Paul's letter to
the Galatians,
a vellum leaf
with early
English
illumination
(IC.56a)

27
The same page
of the vellum
copy of the
Lambeth
Palace New
Testament,
also
illuminated in
England

mordetis et comeditis: videte ne ab
inuicem consumamini. Dico aut in cristo.
Spiritu ambulate: z desideria carnis
non pficietis. Caro enim concupiscit
aduersus spiritu: spirit? aut aduersus
carnem. hec enim sibi inuicem aduersan-
tur: ut non quecunq vultis illa facia-
tis. No si spiritu ducemini: non estis
sub lege. Manifesta sunt aut opera
carnis: que sunt fornicatio immundi-
cia impudicicia luxuria ydolorum secui-
tus veneficia inimicicie contenciones e-
mulationes ire rixe dissensiones se-
cte inuidie homicidia ebrietates
comessationes z hijs similia: q pdico
vobis sicut pdixi: quonia qui talia
agunt regnu dei non consequentur. Fru-
ctus aut spiritus est caritas gaudiu
pax paciencia benignitas bonitas
longanimitas mansuetudo fides mo-
destia continencia castitas. Aduersus
huiusmodi non est lex. Qui autem
sunt cristi: carnem sua crucifixerunt
cum viciis et concupiscenciis.

Si viuim? spiritu: spiritu z ambu-
lem?. Non efficiamur inanis glo-
rie cupidi: inuicem prouocantes: inuicem
inuidentes. Fratres: z si preoccupat? fu-
erit homo in aliquo delicto: vos q spiri-
tuales estis huiusmodi instruite in spiritu lenitatis: considerans teipm ne z tu
tempteris. Alter alterius onera portate:
z sic adimplebitis legem cristi. Na si qs
existimat se aliquid esse cum nichil sit:
ipse se seducit. Opus autem suum pbet
vnusquisq: z sic in semetipso tantu glo-
riam habebit: z non in altero. Vnusquisq
enim onus suu portabit. Communicet
aut his qui catechizat verbo: z qui
se catechizat in omnibus bonis. Noli-
te errare. De? non irridetur. Que enim
seminauerit homo: hec z z metet. Qui

mordetis et comeditis: videte ne ab
inuicem cõsumamini. Dico aũt i cristo.
Spiritu ambulate: z desideria carnis
non pficietis . Caro enim concupiscit
aduersus spiritu: spirit aũt aduersus
carne. Hec enim sibi inuicem aduersan
tur: ut non quecũq vultis illa facia
tis. Õd si spiritu ducemini: non estis
sub lege . Manifesta sunt autẽ opera
carnis: que sunt fornicatio immundi
cia impudicicia luxuria ydolo2 seruit
tus veneficia inimicicie cõtentiones
emulationes ire rixe dissensiones se
cte inuidie homicidia ebrietates
comessationes z hijs similia: q pdico
vobis sicut pdixi: quonia qui talia
agunt regnu dei nõ consequent. fru
ctus aũt spiritus est caritas gaudiũ
pax paciencia benignitas bonitas
longanimitas mãsuetudo fides mo
destia continẽcia castitas. Aduersus
huiusmodi non est lex . Qui autem
sunt cristi: carnem suã crucifixerunt
cum viciis et concupiscentiis. cap· 6·
Si viuim9 spiritu: spiritu z ambu
lemus. Non efficiamur inanis glo
rie cupidi: inuicem pvocates: inuicem
inuidentes. fratres: z si poccupat9 fu
erit homo i aliquo delicto: vos q spiri
tuales estis huiusmodi instruite i spi
ritu lenitatis: considerãs teipm ne z tu
tempteris. Alter alteri9 onera portate:
z sic adimplebitis lege cristi. Nã si qs
existimat se aliquid esse cu nichil sit:
ipe se seducit. Opus autem suũ pbet
vnusquisq: z sic i semetipo tãtu glo
riã habebit: z nõ i altero. Vnusquisq
enim onus suũ portabit. Comunicet
aũt hijs qui catechizat verbo: ei qui
se catechizat in omnibus bonis. Nolit
e errare. De9 nõ irridetur. Que enim
seminauerit homo: hec et metet. Qui

qui seminat in carne sua · de carne et
metet z corruptiõe: qui aũt seminat
in spiritu: de spiritu metet vitã eternã.
Bonũ aute facientes nõ deficiamus:
tempore enim suo metem9 nõ deficien
tes. Ergo dum tempus habem9 opere
mur bonũ ad oẽs: maxime aute
ad domesticos fidei. Uidete qualibz
litteris scripsi vobis mea manu. Qui
cunq enim volut placere in carne hij
cogunt vos circũcidi: tantũ ut crucis
cristi psecutione nõ paciant. Neq; eni
qui circũcidũtur legem custodiũt: sed
volũt vos circũcidi ut in carne vestra
glorient. Michi aũt absit gloriari
nisi in cruce dni nostri ihesu cristi: per
quẽ michi mũdus crucifixus est: z ego
mũdo. In cristo enim ihesu neq; circũ
cisio aliquid valet neq; pputiũ: sed nõ
ua creatura. Et quicunq hãc regulã
secut fuerint: pax sup illos z misericor
dia z sup israhel dei. De cetero nemo
michi molestus sit. Ego enĩ stigmata
dni ihesu i corpore meo porto. Gratia
dñi nri ihesu cristi cum spiritu vro fres
amen. Explicit epla ad galathas
Incipit argumentũ in epistolã ad ephesios
Ephesij sunt asyani. Hij
accepto verbo veritatis p
stiterũt i fide. Hos collau
dat aplus scribes eis a ro
ma de carcere p tychicũ dyaconũ. Expli
cit argumentũ. Incipit epistola
Paulus aplus cristi
ihesu p voluntate dei
omnibus sanctis qui
sunt ephesi: et fidelibs
in cristo ihesu. Gra
cia vobis et pax a
deo patre nostro: et dño ihesu cristo.
Benedict9 de9 et pater dñi nostri ihesu
cristi q benedixit nos i oĩ benedictoue

Further Reading

Janet Ing, *Johann Gutenberg and his Bible*. New York and London: The Typophiles, 1987

Albert Kapr, *Johann Gutenberg. The Man and his Invention*. London: Scolar Press, 1996

Douglas McMurtrie, *The Gutenberg Documents*. New York: Oxford University Press, 1941

S. H. Steinberg, *Five Hundred Years of Printing*, revised edition. London: The British Library, 1996

Margaret B. Stillwell, *The Beginning of the World of Books, 1450 to 1470*. New York: Bibliographical Society of America, 1972

Acknowledgments

Koichi Yukishima, Shuji Tomita of the Maruzen Co. (Tokyo), Masatoshi Shibukawa and Keio University Library (Fig. 12)
Ursula Baurmeister and the Bibliothèque Nationale de France (Fig. 4)
Biblioteca Pública, Burgos, and Vicent García editores, Barcelona (Fig. 17)
Eva Hanebutt-Benz, Roland Kany and the Gutenberg-Museum, Mainz (Figs 6 and 8)
Holger Nickel and the Staatsbibliothek zu Berlin (Fig. 15)
David Zeidberg, Alan Jutzi and The Huntington Library, California (Fig. 14)
William Stoneman and The Scheide Library, Princeton, New Jersey (Figs 19-21)

The National Library of Scotland (Fig. 22)
The Provost and Fellows of Eton College (Fig. 18)
The Master and Fellows of Trinity College, Cambridge (Fig. 5)
His Grace the Archbishop of Canterbury and Lambeth Palace Library (Fig. 27)

Half title: *detail of 7*

Endpapers: *detail of 6*

Back cover: *detail of 14*

Front cover: *as 13*

ISBN 0-7649-0324-1
Pomegranate Catalog No. A878

Designed and typeset in Monotype Centaur by Roger Davies, Pleshey, CM3 1HT UK
Colour Origination by York House Graphics, Hanwell

Printed in Italy by Artegrafica, Verona